"The language, the invention, the imagination, and the sheer fun of his poems are astounding."

     —Charles Simic

"Dean Young's poems are as entertaining as a three-ring circus and as imaginative as a canvas by Hieronymus Bosch. He is one of the most inventive and satisfying poets writing today."

     —American Academy of Arts and Letters

"Dean Young challenges the reader to hang on as he jigs from one poetic style to another and sets a wondrous course across a Duchampian landscape."

     —*Chicago Tribune*

SHOCK BY SHOCK

ALSO BY DEAN YOUNG

Three Poems

Bender

Fall Higher

The Art of Recklessness

The Foggist

31 Poems

Primitive Mentor

embryoyo

elegy on toy piano

Ready-Made Bouquet (U.K.)

Original Monkey

True False

Skid

First Course in Turbulence

Strike Anywhere

Beloved Infidel

Design with X

DEAN YOUNG
SHOCK BY SHOCK

COPPER CANYON PRESS

PORT TOWNSEND, WASHINGTON

Cover art: Laurie Saurborn, *The Birth of Flight*, 2014. Giclée print from film negative, 8 × 10 inches.

Copper Canyon Press is in residence at Fort Worden State Park in Port Townsend, Washington, under the auspices of Centrum. Centrum is a gathering place for artists and creative thinkers from around the world, students of all ages and backgrounds, and audiences seeking extraordinary cultural enrichment.

LIBRARY OF CONGRESS CATALOGING-IN-PUBLICATION DATA

Young, Dean, 1955–
    [Poems. Selections]
    Shock by shock / Dean Young.
        pages ; cm
    ISBN 978-1-55659-431-1 (cloth : alk. paper)
    I. Title.

PS3575.O782A6 2015
811'.54—dc23

                                    2015027371
                        98765432 first printing

Copper Canyon Press
Post Office Box 271
Port Townsend, Washington 98368
www.coppercanyonpress.org

for David Breskin

Joe Di Prisco

Laurie Saurborn

& Michael Wiegers

as a golden mouth lightly touches

        a forehead fashioned of cobwebs,

     I seemed to have entered an unsuspected portal.

           KENNETH PATCHEN

CONTENTS

SHOCK BY SHOCK

Could Have Danced All Night

The wolf appointed to tear me apart
is sure making slow work of it.
This morning just one eye weeping,
a single chip out of my back and
the usual maniacal wooden bird flute
in my brain. Listen to that feeble howl
as if having fangs is something to regret,
as if we shouldn't give thanks for blood
thirst. Even my idiot neighbor backing out
without looking could do a better job,
even that leaning diseased tree or dream
of a palsied hand squeezing the throat but
we've been at this for years, lying exposed
on the couch in the fat of the afternoon
staring down the moon among the night blooms.
What good's a reluctant wolf?
The other wolves just get it drunk
then tie it to a post. Poor pup.
Here's my hand. Bite.

Unlikely Materials

Continued soggy in the personal today
although two strangers smiled at me,
one because I couldn't open a plastic bag
either, the other because I stepped aside
as if I was holding the door for her
even though it was an automatic door.
The peaches, first of the season, were tiny
and powerful as baby rattlesnakes.
A branch had fallen on the driveway
by the time I got home like a friendly
arm over a shoulder so I sat in the car
listening to the rain try to find its melody,
not wanting to flunk my student for not
turning in his 20 pages on clouds
after promising he would. You're singing,
I say every class. Even in the heart
of an artichoke, there's probably a god.
Energy is stored in the triphosphate bond
then released when that bond is broken.
Is that why everything is so hard?
One big pearl, said the Buddha, then glanced
shyly about to make sure no one
understood him. We know only that the spirit
is not matter, is not sap stilling in the veins
or even mist coalesced of the last breath,
sang Orpheus before being torn apart.

Street of Blind Knife Throwers

One of the best I've known couldn't
get out of bed without a drink or a smoke.
Some carry swords purely for show.
Many come and go talking in non sequiturs.
For a while, one who rhymed was so uptight
rhyme was ruined for the rest of us but
of course there's a world in a handful of dust.
One thought she was a genius for putting
9 commas in a row. Do not be too quick
to embrace an alternative energy source,
let fracking be your guide. Some things
can only be found when you hide. Sometimes
it's like a fistfight to decide who's
the biggest pacifist. At dawn the traveler
makes his farewell song. Is there anything
duller than an inaugural poem? One couldn't
write about his father not coming back
from Vietnam without a word list. Do not
underestimate the power of artificial flowers.
Euripides, strawberries, mist. Hence
his tears. The liner notes say that sound
is the cellist scraping his metal chair.
Amplify the accident. Petrify the whim.
The smell is the emergency brake.
Play vigorously with the lid closed, wrote
Satie in the margin. As if about to be devoured
by ants, recommended Lorca before being shot
in the head. Blood, sugar, gasoline
and spot remover. Some come directly
from the sky, others take more circuitous
routes. Like a red rose and just as corny,

one makes every mouth a wound. A few,
in plastic, lie upon the caskets. Clock face,
palace, pavement, crown, all fall down.
Some strain their thorny leashes, others
just bow down.

Crash-Test Dummies of an Imperfect God

Because we're so stupid,
the prizes in Cracker Jack are now paper
so they can be swallowed. No getting
within a hundred feet of Stonehenge because
everyone wants to hack off a souvenir
and the way home is clogged to one lane
so whoever wants to can stare into a pothole
until coming up with a grievance. I'd vote
the greatest accomplishment of mankind
is the pickle spear. God created paradise
to tell us Get out! which is why we probably
created God who doesn't much like being created
by such ilk as us. No wonder it's pediatrics
every morning and toxicology by happy hour.
Is it all just in the mind, the dirty dirty mind?
Maybe God tried to turn you into a dumpster
so you could be lifted by the truck's hydraulic
arm and banged empty. Maybe a sno-cone
so you could be sticky-sweet and dropped.
Maybe a genital-faced bivalve to be dashed
with Tabasco and eaten whole
or to his glory, produce a pearl.

Romanticism 101

Then I realized I hadn't secured the boat.
Then I realized my friend had lied to me.
Then I realized my dog was gone
no matter how much I called in the rain.
All was change.
Then I realized I was surrounded by aliens
disguised as orthodontists having a convention
at the hotel breakfast bar.
Then I could see into the life of things,
that systems seek only to reproduce
the conditions of their own reproduction.
If I had to pick between shadows
and essences, I'd pick shadows.
They're better dancers.
They always sing their telegrams.
Their old gods do not die.
Then I realized the very futility was salvation
in this greeny entanglement of breaths.
Yeah, as if.
Then I realized even when you catch the mechanism,
the trick still convinces.
Then I came to in Texas
and realized rockabilly would never go away.
Then I realized I'd been drugged.
We were all chasing nothing
which left no choice but to intensify the chase.
I came to handcuffed and gagged.
I came to intubated and packed in some kind of foam.
This too is how ash moves through water.
And all this time the side door unlocked.
Then I realized repetition could be an ending.
Then I realized repetition could be an ending.

The Death of André Breton

Only page 200 and already Breton's
finding it impossible to reconcile
life to his dream. If only he could feel
my old dog drinking from his cupped palms.
If only some fog were still alive in him,
he wouldn't be making the marvelous
so uninhabitable even Desnos with his cortex
of starfish expelled. Forgive us, André
and forgive yourself. We tried to dictate
a nocturnal manifesto to the bomb blast
but children's laughter kept ripping
camellias in our darkness, the tips
of our bodies turning green. Do you think
the dirt disapproves of anything? Nothing rots
underground, the brain seeps autumnal garlands
like those late Sinatra songs where he's hungover
just enough to sound husky and roughed up
like a butterfly caught in a downpour.
Yes, the height of civilization is still
guided tours of prisons so surely now
is no time to be serious. Look how frantically
the hearts of those roses beat. Look
at those party boats in the sky. Yes,
we all come into this world through a wound.
The soft thing rips, monsters arrive
with the light and what a struggle
just to stand up while the clouds break,
crickets quiet, flames come to the tongue
and the thorax is ransacked by bells bells bells.

Heavy Lifting

It doesn't matter that the robot
in the bathroom won't dispense you
any paper towels or the monkey
in the lab acts like you don't exist.
Your shadow knows better.
Your shadow knows nothing exists
which is why it makes you
many-minded as a pinwheel
in a wind tunnel.
It's always afterward for your shadow.
Always before.
In the meantime, and it's always meantime,
a lot of trash piles up
but look at your shadow crouching like a wolf
while you clip your toenails.
Look how it leaps the stairs.
I'm not here to help you with your shadow,
I'm here to help your shadow with you.
It loves the pyramids you doodle
during the meeting while you're being screwed.
Certainly it wants you on a looser leash
and when you're falling asleep,
it teaches you to climb a tower or tree
so you can look down upon yourself,
your bed, the house, Earth.
Easy, huh?
You'll never be minuscule again.

Not Trying to Win No Prize

When I listen to rain, I give up,
especially the early acoustic stuff.
I ain't no monkey but I got a bell on my bike.
How do you mend a broken etcetera?
This is me giving up.
Still the great pulse of pointlessness
drives me forward although I don't know
what qualifies as forward. A flower?
Death? There's a waterfall between us
that can drown out almost any scream
all to the good. I don't know if you're ready
to be confronted with the small black screws
that fell out of you in the library
but who is? Now I want to say
something about giraffes, their long blue tongues
and what was thought until recently
their total silence.

Glorious Particles in the Atmosphere Aflame

My dog loves being airborne.
She leaps over the coffee table onto the couch.
Never will we be sealed in the necropolis again.
Leaps when she infers a biscuit.
A walk. A piece of crystal broken off
from the original idea of light.
Then she gets introspective and lies on the rug.
We're surrounded by books and in each a poet
holds the sun in some sort of basket
then his or her skull starts to glow.
One more minaret to the mind.
When my dog misses her puppies,
she gets the walrus from the toy box
and finishes ripping its white fluffy guts out.
Look, she says, snow. Even my dog
is more creative than me
although I make a wicked margarita.
The secret is capsicum.
The secret is drinking from a test tube.
Something's just exploded in outer space
but don't worry, by the time it reaches us
we'll long be ash by other means.

The Usual

Even though I screwed a No Soliciting
sign to the front door, here come
the short-sleeved white shirts to tell me
about the end of the world. I love
the end of the world but they won't
even entertain giant grubs erupting
from the earth mutated by bomb testing.
There's a single genetic switch
that will give us all superpowers
and I can already feel myself stretch
and hover while one of them sails away
in a thimble in his own eye and the other
just looks piqued. They don't want to watch
the movie where the couple first meets
and immediately their shadows start
making out. They don't want a slip
of pickle juice in their Bloody Marys
which they don't want either and my cat,
the devil incarnate, freaks them out
eviscerating his toy mouse. Okay, I say,
see all that bamboo growing wild outside?
Let's cut it down and make a raft.
I'll get the machetes.

How I Got Through My Last Day on the Transplant List

I spent half the afternoon trying
to float my head 3 inches above my shoulders
then a postcard of some lava arrived.
I knew my friends were in Hawaii

but what were they trying to do to me?
Who knows how I spent the morning?
Unearthing errant chips or just holding
out a burning branch? Someone needed to do

some serious alphabetizing around here.
Could molten rock possibly be so red,
so fleet? Could my head just float off?
A beard clung to my cheeks by tiny grappling hooks

while I sat on the back stairs of the universe,
as far as my cord would go, somewhere
between Jupiter and Mars who are so far apart
they can't hear the rotten names they call

each other which is the only reason
the galaxy isn't in even smaller bits.
Obviously, I had work to do. I had
tax forms, my box of crayons, a rubber

tomahawk, lots of wing dust. When
you're waiting for a new heart,
you're waiting for someone to die.

Eternally the Sky Calls to Us

It was odd to be able to check out
a cadaver from the library. You went
for a book about how to make a sturdy
kite out of pizza boxes and barbed wire
and next to the recent acquisitions
was propped a medium-sized somewhat shrunken
professorial-looking fellow. The librarian
behind the desk couldn't move her face either
as you produced your card and slung the thing
over your back. It sure wasn't the shield
of Achilles but surprisingly it smelled okay,
kinda like a gardenia in a shoe or a piece
of wedding cake long frozen because
the groom drove off a cliff on the way
to church. Just wait till those bastards
see this, you think walking to the park
where all your previous kites were torn apart
by screaming hawks and angels aflame.

The Late Work of Pinkham Ryder

My old friend stopped by
to see how my procedure had gone.
I'd arranged all the green rocks
of my collection, mostly fluorite,
at one end of the table
and was winding up the robots at the other.
Not bad for someone whose left hand
occasionally slapped himself
but I was in no mood to reminisce
now that the only decent café in town
had burned down. You had to drive carefully
in that area because engineering students
now wandered around like smoked bees
without a hive. I myself had to stare
at a dandelion blowing out its brains
to steady myself. Not that I'd mention it
to my friend who's one of those people
who think it's an emergency when you pee
purple or your head's even a tiny bit
on fire or you're talking in your sleep
which, by the way, I'm doing now
not that that inhibits my field command.
Robots, attack!

Three-Hearted Poem

There's a slight knock at the door
and when I open it, there's a mailman-
sized moth. That's how I know I've shrunk
even more than the last time when
a blue cloud told me I was drunk,
I was always drunk so from now on
that door's gonna have to answer me.
And you know what? Ain't nothing
I need to ask. Not if there're any more
cashews left. Not if there's a god.
A few years back when I was among some humans,
we all agreed it was a terrible idea
to drop acid and go to chemistry lab.
So we did. Of course it got personal.
Then later when my father was dying
and it was my turn to watch, I could see
even that wasn't going to be easy.
Even then they wouldn't let you smoke.
Even then the staples holding on your face hurt.
Even then you could be entirely mistaken
about your place in the sky.

Success Story

You've survived the giant spiders.
You've survived disco and your mother,
Robert Frost and the little bits
of yourself cut off and cultivated
in petri dishes then released into the wilds.
Sure you've had your brushes
with suspicious minestrones
and that wasn't just a squirrel
you were watching watching you
nor was it a dream,
it was hardly even darkness.
Great shadow forces are congregating
in Northampton. Maybe your pet bird
will return. Just look at my ankle
and see what can be endured.
When I was dying, I didn't bother
filing my income taxes.
They came and got me anyway
with their myriad-fingered resuscitation devices
so I paid a chain-smoker $900
so I'd have to pay them only 9 grand
and now here I am, unmanacled before you
so hang in there. Turkey burgers
are surprisingly tasty and economical
when incorporated with onions and mushrooms.
Ditto watching the sunset
from the jaws of the leviathan.
Once I found a perfectly intact
porcelain doll's head in a wad of kelp.
Once I took an umbrella to a knife fight
and came out with a goldfish.

No one believing you is a symptom
of telling the truth.

Another Original Monkey

I wanted to get across the bridge
but you said we had to find the monkey first.
A billboard practically lost in fog
advertised what?
while the ocean unrolled itself
and you couldn't see what was written on it either
but the monkey just came out of the trees
and took my hand
like we'd been friends since
the soul finally made itself visible
and was bleeding from the mouth
with Xs in half of its 7 eyes.
The monkey's hand was soft
but not moisturized like a hand reaching from the grave
or cold like rain on ice.
It wasn't a dead cat under the porch
your mother paid you a buck to drag out
and when you grab it by the tail the fur slips off.
It wasn't a rubber hand under the pillow
when you stayed with your friend in Chicago
or the same rubber hand you put in his refrigerator
starting this whole rubber hand business.
It wasn't a memory
or a cobweb the size of your face
upon which it was.
Neither the dismembered hand of a murdered pianist
crawling through the late-night movie
you're watching because you can't sleep
hooked up to your own horror movie
only it's not a hospital or laboratory
but a cloud jagged with lightning,

molecules crashing into each other fleeing each other
and all you are is a head
in fact all you are is a skein of brain tissue
bubbling in a jar of blue fluid
on an alien planet ruled by giant
mitochondrial-looking pieces of algae
and their slave waterfalls.

Caruso on Pluto

Part of me still believes
it's possible to breathe
fire. Miles Davis can't be the only one.
I've positioned myself close
to where the membrane's thinnest
not just for the rip
but also the merriment
like when through the flimsy
exam-room walls I can hear someone else
getting the bad news, hear the shrinkage
in their voices and the mice coming out.
I'd gotten some confusing test results,
turns out my blood's not blood at all,
too green, too miasmic and lupine
so my cover's blown
like during the psychological experiment
when they give you chocolate kisses
for upping the voltage into your monkey
and I said I'd rather have the shocks for myself.
Besides, my monkey sure looked like
he could use a sweet.
That was before coming here,
before the surgeries and Tomaz
mutilating the pizza with a fork
then things got really weird
in the cowboy movie that wasn't
a cowboy movie at all. It was
one of those lost-spaceman flicks
where his crippled spaceship crashes
on some inhospitable Styrofoam rock
but through ingenuity and dumb luck

he survives on a strange root
that cries aloud each time it's cut,
not that anyone needs to be reminded.

Bird-Shaped Cliff

Sometimes I think about climbing
a telephone pole but then what?
Telephone poles now have almost nothing
to do with telephones but I liked
how a curly cord went into the receiver
then a sturdier black wire went into the wall
through the wall out to a pole then
miles and miles of wire pole wire pole
sometimes underground underwater to
whomever you needed who'd dry her hands
thinking Gosh now what or Thank heavens
or Oh no then say Hello as a question
or a lie then the intimate negotiations
and sorry confessions and flat jokes
would take word form from excited electrons
moving through the wire and sometimes
a cowboy would suddenly gallop to town
through dust and cactus Yup a storm's
a-coming to call someone but the fates
intend otherwise because that's what fates
always intend so the cowboy must listen
for the rest of his days to the phone
make a funny insect-performing-Beckett
sound until the operator comes on and says,
Sorry but that calling area's been hit
by the blast and the cowboy thinks,
What blast? What blast? riding off
into the moonlessly blue chaparral.

Crow Hop

I think that crow recognizes me
or at least my spot on the periodic table
between those elements
that only exist for a couple nanoseconds
after being bombarded
with enough energy to light a college town.
Crows act like the moment you turn your back
they'll rifle through your medicine cabinet.
Mine actually is a cabinet,
not a shallow shelf behind the bathroom mirror,
an actual piece of furniture.
Don't even get me started on mirrors.
Mine smokes too much
then tries to turn everything into a staring contest.
You know what you show them crows?
If we all unfurled our own blackly ferruginous wings right now!
You know you can fly, right?
You just flex your knees
and launch yourself into the mulberry trees.

Raft Hidden in Weeds

Personally, I've got my pockets full of rocks.
Got a squeaky shoe.
After nearly 60 years of drumming,
you'd think a little rest would be my due.
My face feels flabby today.
Like it's hooked on wrong.
Like it didn't line-dry right.
Like corvine is its throat.
Well, I like all kinds of music anyway.
Bone-tunes. Cat-on-the-piano.
Such that may absorb gunfire,
such that lie underwater.
And—I only heard it once—
a bell dropped down some stairs.
Kicked actually.
At the bottom wasn't anything.
Does everything have to be about the end of the world?
We all dwell among dandelions and demons.
Snow falls on our bonnets.
The body doesn't lie.
When it wants ribbon, give it ribbon.
When it's time to turn silver,
when it cries in the middle of the cartoon
and bees fly from its hollow trunk,
when it finds a ledge to lie on
and all it wants is crushed ice,
give it some crushed ice.

Blue Mansion

First we're given a menu
of counterproductive choices
because all we want is scrambled.
Then we drive by the unoccupied
blue mansion to look at slides
that look like scattered salt
and listen to how our star will die.
You present me with a book dented
I can tell without asking
from where you knocked your head.
Part of friendship is not asking.
Like when I was on crutches.
Like about your eye.
For my birthday you gave me
an awfully familiar shirt.
I always watch your cat.
You helped me with an immense
box of grapefruit I bought
from a truck driver at the door
who scared me. Still many mummified.
It was winter and when you walked
across the carpet in socks
by the time you got to the other side,
you were charged.
Imagine walking straight
into a blue mansion.
There was a tree with cedar waxwings
so tipsy from eating overwintered, fermented
crab apples, I could touch them.
It won't explode.
It'll expand then collapse

and everything will be all at once
at least in this part of the galaxy.
Imagine walking through room
after room calling
to the no ones home.

Eternal Is Our Journey, Brief Our Stopover

I arrived in this warbling city
of lavish poisons and lavisher antidotes
with nothing but a monkey and now look at me.
Not the outer me holding up this shirt
resisting its restraints, the inner me
where a monkey used to sing sad lowland
songs about a mysterious backstage pass
that allowed us access to the puppets
being varnished. Birds of disturbing plumage
perched on my shadow like my own personal
hood ornaments. Of course homeless, of course
famished and barnacled. Of the many things
I have not seen at midnight, don't count how
a soul flees from a ransacked body
or digs in its claws. I've wanted
only to be astonished which is why
during the April blizzard I went looking
for blossoms even if that meant looking
into my own palms. You think it's death
I'm talking about? You think it's that simple
to have a piece of yourself washed away
and something else put back not that I know
which is which any more than the wind knows
if it's coming or going. Sometimes I get so
distracted with unwrapping the bandages
I wonder if my monkey was ever real
just as doubtlessly he wonders about me.

Exit Strategies

Second to last day of November
2014, a year I can almost admit
to surviving. In an airport
in North Carolina, Laurie looks up
from her phone and says, Sad news.
No one is allowed to live forever
so that part isn't a surprise.
The whole flight back I try to block out
the kid screaming behind me
even though he is me.
The stewardess tries her toy-plane
trick followed by the beverage cart.
I wish I was an ancient Chinese poet
so drunk even the moon seems sober.
I wish my mind was a flower.
Carry me oh carry me home.

A Banner Day in the Boonies

At first when the cookie said,
Today will be encouragement blossom day
I thought it was just a cookie talking
but then my dog compliments me
on my composure around squirrels.
By the time I get to work after admiring
some eternal road construction, the claimants
like unvexed molecules have canceled
each other happily out, producing
water vapor and a substrate of gold ore.
At the sub shop, a guy with one blue eye
winks it and says, Twice the meat free!
When I walk into a wall, the wall
apologizes. I remember my friend's poem
about finding a bullet in a bag of popcorn.
I remember a poem about almost being murdered
by a sunset. Kenneth's hand is still on
my shoulder. I remember not being beaten
by my parents so I leave immediately
for the sea, go up to the ticket counter
and say, I need to get to the sea
and a woman dressed like an ensign
of a retro-futuristic soft-core spaceship
says, Of course you do,
says, giving me free upgraded legroom,
You're nearly there.

Rites of Spring

Sometimes the heart must be torn out,
sometimes protected with thorns.

One woman's being eaten by a flower.
No, she's being lifted from the grave.

One heart is almost never enough,
a man is arguing with the music
but the music always wins. Inside

the electric bell, the hammer's to
and fro is produced by magnetic action
but inside the body are other, quiescent

going wacka wacka forces.
To be hungry is to be alive,

to be alive is to be on fire,
to be on fire is to have a mind.

It's not just pain chasing the flock
which turns all at once as I do toward you.
Let dissonance be our recognition,

let a burning scarecrow be our guide.
Woe unto anyone who doubts this meadow.
One man is battling his shadow.

A woman with one wing tramples the earth.
Sometimes the heart just beats itself apart.

Sky Below

Maybe it doesn't hurt to be a constellation.

Or a swan even though it takes all day
to get out of the shell. Trees seem okay
unless something happens to them and something
is always happening to trees. Our shield
against the cruelty of this world might
as well be moth-wing dust so it can take
some resistance like not getting on a plane
you're supposed to. Everyone's expecting
a lot from you and the boss's disappointment
can make the cupcakes after the meeting
taste like lint. It's common to feel ruined.
God says, You call that a garden?
Things like that happen to the mind
and the body can't believe it. A sailboat
leans way over to hurry but sometimes sinking
is fastest. We love each other but then
it's the same circular bullshit—the yard
fills with lilies of the valley then
the dog rips open the couch's throat.
Things like that happen to the body
and the mind can't believe it. Maybe
you look back at the house you just left
and people are dancing in devil masks.
It's okay to want to let everything go,
to lie down in the sky. It's normal
your mother gives you migraines and to wake
in the middle of the night unable

to tell if you're upside down.

Flash Powder

Tonight when I look out the hotel window,
the bells inside me are quiet but
they start up again walking through the park
to the statue of the sun stepping on
a giant crab. Sunset wears a crown
like a wound wears a crown.
Even then the gods are at work.
The eyes see something beautiful beyond,
the shells of attending snails twirling
like galaxies made into mathematical formulas
like flames trying to become a rose. It all
makes sense, promise the physicists
piling on more and more dark matter
like in a Lou Reed song. Please please
please, peals the oblongata.
What the fuck with everything.

A Student Comes to My Office

Okay, you'd think I'd be satisfied scaring
his whole class with Lorca's biography,
some trivia about bacteria, Dionysus's
treatment of disbelievers but this kid
keeps trying to keep his Euclid-head on
even though a bike wreck made him miss
his chem test and now he looks around
like his eyes want to get away from his thoughts.
Looks at what? Maybe the photo of me
in Fort Worth, fracking capital of the world,
beside a flying book. Maybe the 10,000
slim volumes of verse about tapeworms
in the heart and goats singing in rivers
of blood or maybe the plastic Pegasus foal
hatching on my desk and who doesn't need
a little help? It hurts getting out of an egg,
hurts having the same light inside your liver
as a hyena, same rosebush in the aorta.
So maybe some panic goes out of him but not much.
It's raining and when it rains in Texas
every insect pupates and thinks, Now's my chance!
so it's like being in a womb of sharks
just trying to eat your liverwurst sandwich
by the turtle pond full of scummy lotus flowers
commemorating all those people shot
by a sniper in the clock tower.

Light-Bringers

Maybe no one escapes. Lorca rubs
his hand across the misted window:

they're coming. Maybe it's a waltz,
maybe a flamenco. Mayakovsky
wipes away some frost: they're here.

Spilled red wine stains a letter. A boot
crushes a doll's head. Maybe

a falling feather's veronica enough.
Once my mother was a child playing
a child's violin then they used a motorized

crank to lower her in and the ground covered
itself like a mouth filling with wildflowers.

Then snow and whatever was left alive
burrowed deeper. Maybe a river meanders
because it knows its destination.

Remember the last time we visited the old man?
He thought we were robbers until

you gave him the strawberries.

Why I Haven't "Outgrown Surrealism" No Matter What That Moron Reviewer Wrote

I still love the sound of breaking,
the tear of the page, fruit that splits
when it's ripe. Not sticks and string
and a 30-page instruction manual
when I need a kite, when I need
a dragon in the sky. More and more
only the irrational holds me
to this earth not that I need Apollo
knocking my helmet off to tell me so.
Give me a bird crashing a window
in the darkness of daylight, a red
wine stain on my good white shirt
and a dog park where we scatter Chloe,
some blowing back on our shoes in a very
Chloe-like manner, two living dogs
coming up to us wagging hard enough
to levitate in recognition. The body
is a vessel of flame-flicker
and even in dreams I say my love's
name so picture me for verisimilitude
made entirely of sunflowers but keep
the long scar in the center of my chest,
under it a grim doctrine frolics
on a dissecting table. I who have been
restored by cardiac shocks, dropped
into morning wanton and struck.

Another Lethal Party Favor

I was being ushered somewhere to be beaten
when I ran into my old friend Harry.
He looked slicked down like he'd had help
licking his wounds and when I told him where
I was going, he said, Ha, they don't even know
how to beat a fly there. That's Harry for you.
Don't let him see you dragging your trash
to the curb because he'll have to produce
a bigger heap, carry it on his back even if
his chin almost scrapes the ground like
a dung beetle's. Tell him about your heart
transplant and he'll say, Didn't know
you had a heart. Lately he's been concentrating
on contemporary poetry of all things,
kinda a relief like if Hitler had stayed
interested in painting more than politics.
Besides, it was a beautiful day to be beaten,
one of those spry spring afternoons you feel
you could talk to a daffodil and the daffodil,
full of its own problems, would nonetheless
accompany you into the dark cave of your own
skull like a torch held up by a villager
intent upon burning down the castle.

Speech Therapy

The ugly duckling remained ugly
its whole life but found others
as ugly as itself. I guess that's the message.
Smoke rises from the heads in the backyard.
Do you think if I hang around long enough
someone will proffer me a muffin,
one skulking shadow to another?
Soon, my shoes will be part of the populous dump.
Have I learned all the wrong lessons,
the ones you shouldn't know until
the last dew-clogged lawn is mowed
and the sun goes down on the ruined battlements?
Why was I given a toy train if not
to stage stupendous wrecks? Sure,
I can walk by the sea holding my hand
with as much melancholy as the next fellow,
substituting the cries of the slammed waves
for the droll adumbrations of distraught
goons, the day taking on the sheen
of a stone removed from the mouth
and skipped between breakers jubilant and sunk.

Surgery in Air

By the time I get outside,
my wife's smiling because the estimate
is not any worse so I say,
What are you strangers doing
on my boat in the middle of the night?
I can see my grasshopper head
in the tree-man's mirror shades.
He looks like he manages ex-cons well
and knows what weeping black sap means.
My wife looks like a swan
who could chuck a pretty good javelin
even though since the Greeks
it hasn't been a girl-event.
On one of her chamomile shoulders
is a tattoo eye. There's no eye on the other,
a long story and when bits bubble up
after a couple drinks, she pushes
its head back underwater.
No one thinks I'm funny.
In fact they both look bug-wise at me
like I know nothing of a limb falling
on a house, taking along some power lines.
Like I'm an escapee from midnight
who should get out of the sun.
Like I'm not the one warning everyone
about the multimillion-dollar debris
hurtling toward us from outer space,
like I'm not the one paying for all this.

Underground River

Once my darling agreed
to come home with me,
don't laugh,
I had a foolproof story
if she forgot what was happening
when the silk kimono ripped
or the chicken seemed raw
or my dog wouldn't shut up about his operation
or the cuckoo clock with the bird busted
looked like it was sticking out a splinter
or the place smelled like a troop of strawberries
had galloped over a hill and been massacred
or thought I was trying to trick her into some play
where she'd have branches glued all over her
or listen to the entire remastered King Crimson back catalogue,
I tell her about animals who lived so long underground
maybe because their pond fell down an earthquake-opened shaft
or lava welded shut their hiding cave,
their bodies grow translucent
and absorb their eyes down to sensitive nubs
and elongate their ears
and make electrical their noses
even mutating thready dish-like appendages
to broadcast and pick up the sorts of signals
on which all species depend
even as in our case creatures made entirely of light.

Grasshopper in a Field Being Mowed

Sometimes I see things.
Even when I open my eyes,
all of them.
Sometimes even when I don't see things,
I bump into them.
Which hurts. Variously.
Like a character in a novel finding out
what the reader's known from page 1.
Or stepping on a blop of conditioner in the shower.
Or electricity in fur.
Or raspberries.
Syringes.
Sarcophaguses.
Like sunshine.
Like a little girl crying in the baloney aisle.
Like the lighting in the baloney aisle.
Like the diverting sound of the word *abattoir.*
Say it, *abattoir.*
Which isn't a type of swan.
I'm not sure I want to live forever anyway
even given all the collage materials.
The pizzas in piazzas
amid the fluttering skirts.
Too expensive.
Too many biopsies.
Too many heat waves.
Too many marriages to mist.

Oracle

I find myself more and more among
those marginal characters who seem intent
on getting nothing done, decommissioned hussars,
jilted maids-in-waiting or fauns even,
all woolly from the waist down realizing
their eon's over, no one believes in them
anymore and if you asked, Heck, they'd say,
we never much believed in ourselves.
It all happened so long ago, the storming
of the prison, the invention of happy gas,
the marriage of the sun and moon, epic
swings of ballyhoo and swoon. Suddenly
a lady might need her petticoat removed,
the band would play until the fuzz arrived,
and faeries were almost safe in piano bars.
But the certainties of any age must be shoved aside
to allow the next loud, thunking youth
its anthems and wars, its sputter and splatter.
Such has been muttered since the end
of time and will be muttered more while
the world stays stitched with golden rays
and each finds her own way out.

Everyday Escapees

My poor students, all I ask of them
is to grow antennae, lie down with lava
and rise with snow, grow tongues from
their math assignments and no, Melissa

your mother won't approve of a bioluminescent
smear on your communion dress. The world fidgets
in uneasy relation to our statements about it
nevertheless producing silver

buds from ragged limbs like the luster
in late Rat Pack songs. Finally,
when I got off the sixth floor, I felt
like I was discharged into the sky

and aren't we all pedestrians of air?
Doesn't it feel all wrong to turn our backs
on the ocean? On an ant? On those Chagall
windows you have to walk through a gantlet

of ancient armor to get to? What was her name,
that night nurse so deft her blood draws
didn't wake me up? Don't get me wrong, I want
to wake up. I want my old dog to show me

all that wolf-light she hides inside
even though she thinks I won't understand,
even though her vet and I conspire
to keep her alive forever.

Singing Underwater

What is poetry anyway? My dream
or yours or amalgam of everyone's?
Oneiric eyeball in a tree's bark
or ordinary gulp of air? The hark,
hark of an afterlife or face-plant
in the mud? No matter how many versions
I read, it ends the same: daisies
on a pile of sand while they're burning
the furniture, scraping the walls,
smashing the crockery as dictated by law.
Do you think nightingales even know
if they're being heard? Divine intervention?
Give me a break. Things happen wrong
all the time: the song is singed, burnt
is fired, the lightbulb goes on in the ghost
story. Some days it's hard to withstand
all the demystification, every angel
an angel of demystification despite
her secret cookie recipe. Is it all
just churched-up box mix, moondust
quackery? Doubtlessly confusion
must be banished although some beguiling
hiss of vagaries should remain to catalyze
the confinement of wonderment glowing
in the test tube somehow cool to the touch,
such brevities that evoke eternity.
Scarecrow with a migraine? Gate unhinged?
Words vanishing as whims but staining
the rib cage I mean page. Thus poetry's
most often ambiguous, conciliatory maybes,
no musts but mists, something between

the strict rules of dominoes and a mind's
high disquiet, a few thank-you notes
written in blood.

Bender

Ever since I lost consciousness,
I keep finding it in the oddest places:
in the barn after the dancers turned to chaff,
in bits of chintz, corn husk, phosphenes of dream
that bob up like newts taking drinks of air.
It's okay, there's nothing so adored
as what's lost, more interrogated
than what's found, the silver sliver
plucked out, melted down for the ongoing ingot
of life's bulk as counterweight
to days just whirs and spinouts,
hiccups and coughs into bleached handkerchiefs.
I mean something thorny to knock your head against
like a banana tree although I've never seen one,
might be a bush for all I know.
A little knowing goes a long way
but not-knowing reaches universe's end.
The world is trivial, is trivia.
In its window snow is always falling.
Cephalonomancy is divination
by roasted goat head. A black bear
may be brown, a brown black. One scavenges,
one attacks which makes all the diff
if you should run or play stiff. Each kiss
is further predicament, the star-shaped seeds
drop into your palm, the ta-dum of a child's drum
arterial with the undergirding of some song
like a series of likenesses that will vanish
into like into like into like into like
those squares of sod laid down upon
this scorched earth so lay thee down, my darling.

What if there's only the long plunge
into a sleep there's no waking from?
What if it makes no difference,
the white suit or the black, surfeit
or lack, peacocks on the mansion's lawn
or bioluminescent smear in the summer dark,
marble gods shattered and cavorting
or stations of the cross. Nada, nada, nada.
What wages did I expect anyway? There are storms
so strong nothing grows back and nothing's
been here from the start and will be long
after we're gone. We cast a small circle
of light outside of which wolves revolve
in a slightly larger circle outside of which
orbit what wolves fear: housing developments,
freeways, us, so no wonder our pastures
overlap and who knows whose angel you're
wrestling with. All is vibrating cloud,
a movement from chorale to single voice
like the reverse of the Reformation's austerity
to the baroque, the shift from scene-filling
bystanders to lone rake in the fracas of uncertain
progress and more uncertain end although
I probably have this all mixed up
…and here the station changes itself
as we round this jagged edge of fog,
local dialects of rain that drench and evaporate
without words. What bird was that that never came back?
A lark? Must we now live without that part
of our shadow? I guess we will all be warbled
elsewhere. Somehow we keep departing without
ever having arrived, stretching the taffy
of our lives, losing each other, coming ashore
naked of all but our wits. Must I always be

one of those dim heroes who doesn't realize
all he needs is to hold out a blossom sprig,
not make a speech with his head on fire
with a weasel concealed under his cloak
tearing out his heart. Maybe all the kingdom
ever is is honeycomb in a hollow stump.
Probably it was downpour enough letting
the needle drag through the last endless
groove of *Kind of Blue* when I still had
a record player. No need to sit on the roof
throwing bottles in the street for the sound
of breaking glass, for the storm. I started this
innocently enough with a few primary colors
and the capacity to lie that kept catching
up to me until surpassing me and I became
what the lie told, a hunch half myth,
half dumb ditty like I was the root cause
of all this ache and misunderstanding,
me who chewed up the rain hat, substituted
sugar for salt. Probably a virus, said one
cardiologist. Your father, said another
while I sat on a gurney in a paper gown
wondering what those dark sparks in the mirror were
while those around me filled the unforgiving
60 seconds with screeching and slamming
on the brakes, not that the engine drone
still doesn't set me off, just more likely
a coughing spiel than a plaintive yawp.
I was of the tribe that bit its tongue,
that's what and how we sung. Those in remission
tried to organize those in denial into rubble-
sifting crews, everyone issued popsicles,
encouraged to read in bed until we ruined
our eyes. Chesty swans rumbled across the stage

scaring the faerie prince whose job it was
to catch them. Happy rounds bulged the air
and wolves joined in, the motley horizons
of silly intimations and carnal hijinks,
wrens making homes in fake trees,
piles of cleared brush, dictates that only
acerbated the behaviors they aimed to curtail:
deep-frying, nudity, the resistance
everyone was part of just by breathing.
Some days I miss the swamps out back
of the old homestead, UFO sightings
in the heyday of carpal tunnel syndrome,
the apparatchiks in the frescoed luncheonette
discussing the offhand slips of upper echelon,
my mother knowing who I was or someone like me,
a tally kept naively, the judgment of Santa Claus.
Then we all went to separate islands
like students in a correspondence course.
No one wanted an orange as rhyming material
thus the moon grew wan from overuse. A spiral
spirituality rippled the duck pond
until absinthe was decriminalized and everyone
went Rimbaud. Anachronistically
we were brought up short to the present
in dogcarts, troikas, cabriolets,
age-spotted, waylaid by phantom pains,
mishaps with Krazy Glue, one with a pig valve,
one with a tuck or two, a few self-committed.
Still we knew that alarms of the financial gurus
would not endure. Only glint endures, only bling.
And the contact lens prescription will not endure,
only the blur, the angelic, wanton blur,
the oracle's preferred weather, overcast forecast,
prognostication of muddles for meatheads,

scribbled hearts hermetically sealed,
a baby snake settling in the hand,
accepting its warmth as I would yours
if I ever see you again, if I ever saw you once,
if we ever find our way back home. Come back!
Come back! but nothing comes back, not
the star in the center of the chest, not the river
of bees that was our honeyed bequest, not
the blizzard that was once the mind,
its blaring verifications that life's
a flare, a farce, a kiss from someone in the dark
who thinks she's kissing someone else
you gladly become.

How to Draw a Circle

After we get closer and the frogs quiet,
my dog says, See how the frog quiets
when approached. It's cooling off
as it gets dark as if the earth has realized
light equals heat. We come to a stick
pretending to be a snake. Is it not wise
for a snake to pretend to be a stick?
I keep thinking back to the mean things
said at the meeting, some from my own mouth.
How 40 bucks just vanished from my pocket.
How I doubted that my brother was going to make it
the whole way across the bridge. My dog
has stopped and is looking at me with
a moon in each eye. This is the part
of our walk by the yucca festooned
with Xmas lights and half a mannequin
sticking out of the ground where once
I heard they filmed a commercial
for mayonnaise when my dog asks
what I've learned. Nothing, I don't say
which is the same as saying it.
Good, says my dog. Before enlightenment—
walk the dog. After enlightenment—
walk the dog as we turn toward
the blue door of our own home.

Tomaz, I'm Still among the Living

furiously asserting a few private values
in the face of mass indifference. Sometimes
is it okay to perpetuate the hoax of sincerity
leading a centralized self to commodified
epiphanic end-stops even though the context
is perpetually deferred and everything flies
apart especially me-ee-eee-eeee?
Even here it's snowing but gives up
its pure mission of obliteration before
hitting the ground. My class is so quiet
I don't bother marking absences. End now
I try to stop myself from thinking.
Girls who would be reading Sartre in Berkeley
get snakes tattooed up their asses here.
Each day the recipient of my sexual impulses
grows more beautiful making me glad
I'm a puny demigod otherwise by now
she'd be myrtle or some scarlet, never-
quiet bird. I lie to my cardiologist
about how much wine it takes even though
I wish to provide them with useful data
regarding the three electrodes screwed
into my failing ventricles. They wave a wand
and change my heartbeat from a laptop!
The dog is turning into a cloud. Keats,
my cat, died with my ex, she called so
I could talk to him one last time but
I couldn't manage. Some music is not
to be listened to, just withstood. Is it
okay to be a spotted red leaf on a green bush?
Okay to be, if you have to, a parasite?
Okay to succumb?

Missing Person

Shouldn't someone be wondering
about my whereabouts about now?
I know I am. Must have been in
the vicinity moments ago, there's his frock
still shrugged with warmth, the characteristic
oil spill. Just as well, he was never
one to kiss and tell, twist and yell perhaps
but who needs that? A malaise undone by hiccups
defined the millennium of his peerage past
just as a phonograph needle's scratch
defined the last. Something you could convince
yourself was almost rain. Nothing
a flaming cognac couldn't erase,
nothing a good cry. So let the bells
have their loudmouth say, they always think
it's some religious holiday and everyone's
going to hell unless some friendly angel
intervenes. For the rest of us, the mystery
stays unfinished. Maybe an icicle was the weapon,
maybe you're sleeping with a mole, maybe
you're already dead in yet another pickle
to prod the mulish narrative along
to where it may find us waiting, abashed,
famished and unsolved in the end.

My Wolf Is Bigger Than Your Wolf

I bet you don't even share 10 chromosomes
with your wolf. When my wolf runs off
with my ATM card, she comes back
with the complete works of Kenneth Patchen.
Did you know he wrote many of his finest works
flat on his back in excruciating pain?
What was the heaviest rock ever
put on your chest? Now multiply that
and see if you don't confess
you're a witch even though
your cat ignores you, your mileage
sucks and you never once spit in a cauldron.
See how foolish that is now—
whatever was holding you back
from flying through the zodiac?
You could have known exactly where to dig up
old prescription bottles at the dump
people pay good money for.
You could have known what was inside
the locket recovered from the blast.
Maybe even made Oppenheimer laugh
as Sanskrit blistered his forehead
and helped get Wendy Davis elected
to protect the reproductive rights
of women in Texas. You'd have known
to purify crystals you hold them
under cold running water and hum.
See that tear in the rational?
That's where the miraculous slips in.
Usually it's so small even protozoa
can't squeeze through. That's why
you need a wolf.

Edgework

It's not easy to carry a pyramid
into the sunset with a feather. The sunset
burns the feather, the pyramid crumbles.
It's not easy taking in all the doctor says.
The body is made of brick.
Brick doesn't like being aboveground.
Magnets are useless, peacocks ferocious.
All songs are about falling apart which
provides at least a rhyme for *heart*
because all things must be sung to be
terrible enough. Instructively,
a saint makes an omelet, a saint
holds out her arms and some of the flames
form a crown. The soul leaves the body
with candy-wrapper crinkles. A window
is a sea. A red shirt approximates.
You can see where wings drag in the frost.
You can see faces beneath the ice.
A saint carries a fox under her cape,
on the cape a thousand ears, ichor everywhere.
It's too bright. I can't find my way out.
I can't get drunk enough to warrant
abduction but I can wither yellow,
howl green. Not everyone gets to
lie down in a meadow.

Quiet Grass, Green Stone

I love when out of nowhere

I love when out of nowhere
my cat jumps on me
and my body isn't even surprised.

Me who wants to be surprised by everything

like a dandelion

like a bottle cap

cricket cricket.

I keep waiting for the god under the anthill to speak up.
I keep waiting for the part of the myth
where everyone turns into a different bird
or the reeds start talking
or horses come out of the ocean
in their parliamentary regalia
and cities grow from their hoofprints.
I keep waiting for the bugle
and the jackal-headed god to weigh my heart across the river.

All this daylight in just a few moments
pours itself into darkness. More and more
I'm satisfied with partial explanations
like a fly with one wing, walking.

Emerald Spider between Rose Thorns

Imagine, not even or really ever tasting
a peach until well over 50, not once
sympathizing with Blake naked in his garden
insisting on angels until getting off the table
and coming home with a new heart. How absurd
to still have a body in this rainbow-gored,
crickety world and how ridiculous to be given one
in the first place, to be an object
like an orchid is an object, or a stone,
so bruisable and plummeting, arms
waving from the evening-ignited lake,
head dinging in the furnace feral and sweet,
tears that make the face grotesque,
tears that make it pure. How easy
it is now to get drunk on a single whiff
like a hummingbird or ant, or the laughter
of one woman and who knew how much I'd miss
that inner light of snow now that I'm in Texas.

How to Glow

Either that or the police blotter.
Someone steals a bicycle because he wants
to fly. Wants a new heart. A hive on the porch.
There's someone suspicious in the graveyard
with a torch. What the librarian needs
she cannot say but she's listening
to Bulgarian-language tapes in her car anyway.
Sure beats eating your own pancreas.
The difference between surrealism and dada
like the difference between first- and second-degree
manslaughter hardly matters to most of us.
What you get is a chalk outline of dust,
bells for no reason, mouthfuls of starlight
rusty as blood, gra gra gra grape-stems
stammering of summer and lots of dreams
on paper like in analysis and graduate school.
The difference between graduate school and analysis
is approximately $20,000 although both
occur mainly lying down. The white coats
in the lab peer at the microscope slides
and think it's bad news that the blood
is wolf's blood. Dear Oblivion, I love
your old song. Let a spinning wheel be
my fireplace, let the lit-up nerves of jellyfish
be my Milky Way. The greatest indication of truth
is laughter and maybe now I'm almost ready
to talk to my mother and father. This morning
I have the distinct impression my house
is about to crumble so let rubble be my crown.
Release the hound! What a joke, she's about
a hundred years old and when you look into

her almost-no-one-home eyes, you come to a river
and when you come to that river, you float.

Gizzard Song

Dean, it's Harry. No birds are nesting
in my birdhouses. What could it mean?
I don't know why I answered the phone,
there's already too much going on in
Nacogdoches and not even hello. Harry,
you haven't even asked about my operation.
You sick? No, I had a heart transplant.
They do those with lasers now, right? Lapra-
dazically? No, mine was more complicated, I say,
with knives. Ouch, he deducts, but you must
be okay now. Antlers are growing out of my floors,
a snowman, an evil snowman delivers my mail
and I'm taking so many pills my tongue's purple
and hair's growing out of my forehead so no.
Well, sorry, but you're the only person I
can call. No one knows the habits and inklings
of our winged friends like you. A query about
a foundling fledgling, a moody rooster, an owl
with self-esteem issues, you're the go-to guy.
Even if you feel like a wobbly oblong peg
driven into a wedge of cheddar, you're the guy
who holds it all together not only in avian
affairs but all atmospheric matters: comets
and Martians your métier, angels and even clouds
for crying out loud. What would we do without
you? One day: no birds then stars all falled down
then what? Nothing! The void! The dark maw
of zilch! He was working himself into a fine
fettle and I had to admit, even if he was feeding
you regurgitated worm, he could make you feel
special and all my pains, my multitudinous pains

would shrink to a single whinge like what a word
makes when it's misspelled. Pilgrim, I say,
you need to clear out the old nests, your houses
probably jammed with others' twigs and mud and stuff.
Birds, like the rest of us, like clean starts
and as I spoke I felt my new heart roost deeper
in my chest, fluffing out its blue breast, looking
for something to peck and this is how mercy
and poetry move through the world.

Folklore

You shouldn't have a heart attack
in your 20s. 47 is the perfect time
for a heart attack. Feeding stray shadows
only attracts more shadows. Starve a fever,
shatter a glass house. People often mistake
thirst for hunger so first take a big slurp.
A motorboat is wasted on a hawk just as roses
are on nuclear reactors but I don't want
you to be wasted on me even though
all summer the pool was, I didn't
get in it once. Not in it, not in it
twice. A dollhouse certainly isn't wasted
on a mouse both in terms of habitation
and rhyme. Always leave yourself time
to get lost. 50 cattle are enough
for a decent dowry but sometimes a larger
gesture is called for like shouting
across the Grand Canyon. Get used to
nothing answering back. Always remember
the great effects of the Tang poets,
the meagerness of their wine, meagerness
of writing supplies. Go ahead, drown
in the moon's puddle. Contusions
are to be expected and a long wait
in ICU under the muted TVs advertising
miracle knives and spot removers.
How wonderful to be made entirely
of hammered steel! No one knows why
Lee chose to divert his troops to Gettysburg
but all agree it was the turning point
of the Civil War. Your turning point

may be lying crying on the floor.
Get up! The perfect age for being buried
alive in sand is 8 but jumping up 33, alluding
to the resurrection, a powerful motif
in Western art but then go look at the soup cans
and crumpled fenders in the modern wing:
what a relief. Nearly 80% of the denizens
of the deep can produce their own light
but up here, we make our own darkness.

Rough Drafts

Western wind, rearrange me.
Bail out bliss and crunch it.
I have been half in love with Vickie Dwojak.
The world of dew is the world of doo-doo.
Often I'm permitted to return to Target.
My best robot shoots rockets from its chest.
The earliest form of polo was played with human heads.
Death creeps me out but still I'm attracted
to its tongue in my mouth. I heard a fly buzz
the day I made pickled eggs. Whatever
I'm the child of must be something big.
All the new thinking is about loss
and in this it resembles lots of my old socks.
Something's skipping in the fossil record.
I too hop from branch to branch
with an inordinate fondness for the Beatles.
My pecker's giving me problems.
I wander lonely and out loud,
luckily my sister follows me around with her journal.
I like those old jingles.
Downward on extended wingding.
No ideas but in ka-ching.
It's 12:20 no wait it's 1:15,
what time is it where you are?
I like an explosion that leaves a star.
I like my steak with a good sear.
I hope I end up far from here.
My doctor says I'm ruining my liver.
Take me to a different river.

The Life of the Mind

The best thing about wearing headphones
is my cat thinks "Close to the Edge"
is coming from my head.

Ghost Gust

Before my first heart was cut out,
I never expected the jackal-headed guards
across the river would be such goofballs
or such a flimsy wing would carry me so far
over the volcanoes and palatial department stores
with the robot parking attendants
and caryatids spraying perfume.
Now each bubble in my ginger ale
bursts like the cosmic egg in nothingness
lest I forget I'm but a single atomic thrust
in the shattered void.
I'm ready for my close-up.
I'm ready for my far-away.

If You Can't Levitate, You'd Better Know How to Disappear

I wonder what Zap's doing in San Francisco.
The fog here hardly counts as fog,
it's more what happens inside your head after
a double shift at the drying station
in the plastic-glove factory.
I miss trying to skim flamingo feathers
from the scummy zoo pond beneath the sign
saying not to. A lot of the time
when you wake up from getting stuck
inside a giant clam and think, Sheesh
I'm glad that was just a dream,
something far more insulting to the protocols
of reality crawls from under the bed.
Most days, you can't even expect to put out a bowl
and not have it fill with blood. You can't
hang a wolf costume from a nail and not
get claw marks in the cake. At least
it keeps you alert. My best trick was
to make a flame hop from hand to hand
then up my arm into my hair then ask
in mock despair to be doused with water
which FOOSH goes off like a flashbulb.
My father was the greatest illusionist ever.
Once he took out his own beating heart
and showed it to my mother who was so
used to it, she just kept vacuuming.

Watcher of the Skies

Was the idea to hail the sequined dusk?
To be naked as a horse, a meadow, a glove?
Lightning-struck, wanton and plucked.
Does all music come from hollowness or impact?
To purge, purge, purge
then glut the self with sorrow until it splits
like a pomegranate.
To look on new planets.
To let the dead trees stand,
to continue to sing as a hatchet sings,
as a feather in an owl's wing, silently.
To breathe without stumble.
To develop a stanza with the integrity of a sonnet
but rhymes that don't pounce.
Without any irritable reaching after fact.
To write a play for money,
enter an elephant at the end of the third act.
To nurse a brother, build a soul.
Superannuations of dust.
Compensatory ambergris from the skulls of Greeks.
The idea was the poison in the body
could be drawn into blisters,
the poison in the blood bled out.
To hang from silver nails by vascular gasps.
To soothe the throat, to hope.
The idea was to avoid all excitement.
Years of mercury, laudanum, intoxications on art.
The idea that sexual frustration played a part.
Byron's notion that a nasty review was enough.
A starvation diet,
those last weeks not even reading Fanny's letters

then the bedding burned, walls scraped, all the crockery busted
as dictated by law.
The idea was to live forever.
To have a name writ in water.

This Is the Other Road

When my heart was at last cut out
after stumbling gasping from the shower,
after hours of white rain,
the god was almost satisfied with his wine
the way he wasn't with thistles
in a vacant lot, their feathery
purple ghostheads exploded,
and the ants in their chariots everywhere,
in the refrigerator and our shoes
only interested the god
like a throw of dice in a game
he had no wager in
as did the eclipse that turned the moon
to a maroon party favor for lunatics
and the broken E string
and the voice that keeps singing
not because the god is hungry
or vengeful or horny or particularly
interested in me or you but because
he likes the theater, the gowns and masks,
the rib-cage splitter and ceremonial
reaching into the chest
and a stranger, a boy really,
the heart of a reckless, generous boy
lifted from its cooler
and sutured into a carnal afterlife,
rose by rose, ladder by ladder,
shock by shock by shock.

Believe in Magic?

How could I not?
Have seen a man walk up to a piano
and both survive.
Have turned the exterminator aside.
Seen lipstick on a wineglass not shatter the wine.
Seen rainbows in puddles.
Been recognized by stray dogs.
I believe reality is approximately 65% if.
All rivers are full of sky.
Waterfalls have minds.
We all come from slime.
Even alpacas.
I believe we're surrounded by crystals.
Not just Alexander Vvedensky.
Maybe dysentery, maybe a guard's bullet did him in.
Nonetheless.
Nevertheless
I believe there are many kingdoms left.
The Declaration of Independence was written with a feather.
A single gem has throbbed in my chest my whole life
even though
even though this is my second heart.
Because the first failed,
such was its opportunity.
Was cut out in pieces and incinerated.
I asked.
And so was denied the chance to regard my own heart
in a jar.
Strange tangled imp.
Wee sleekit in red brambles.
You know what it feels like to hold

a burning piece of paper, maybe even
trying to read it as the flame gets close
to your fingers until all you're holding
is a curl of ash by its white ear tip
yet the words still hover in the air?
That's how I feel now.

Acknowledgments

Some of these poems appeared in the following magazines:
*The American Poetry Review, Conduit, Forklift Ohio, Gulf Coast,
H_NGM_N, jubilat, The Massachussets Review, the minnesota review,
Poetry, Poetry Daily, Smoking Glue Gun, The Threepenny Review.*

Thanks to these organizations for their support: the Boomerang
Foundation, Friends for Writers, the University of Texas, and
especially Shifting Foundation.

Thank you to all who contributed to the fund to help defray my
medical costs. It has been a great aid and continues to be so and I
am deeply indebted to your generosity and kind thoughts.

Thanks to Dobby Gibson for his perceptive reading of this book in
an early stage.

About the Author

Dean Young has received support for his work from the National Endowment for the Arts, the John Simon Guggenheim Memorial Foundation, and the American Academy of Arts and Letters. He is currently the William Livingston Chair of Poetry at the University of Texas, Austin.

Poetry is vital to language and living. Since 1972, Copper Canyon Press has published extraordinary poetry from around the world to engage the imaginations and intellects of readers, writers, booksellers, librarians, teachers, students, and donors.

WE ARE GRATEFUL FOR THE MAJOR SUPPORT PROVIDED BY:

THE PAUL G. ALLEN
FAMILY FOUNDATION

CULTURE

Anonymous	Gull Industries, Inc.
John Branch	on behalf of William and Ruth True
Diana Broze	Mark Hamilton and Suzie Rapp
Beroz Ferrell & The Point, LLC	Carolyn and Robert Hedin
Janet and Les Cox	Steven Myron Holl
Mimi Gardner Gates	Lakeside Industries, Inc.
Linda Gerrard and Walter Parsons	on behalf of Jeanne Marie Lee
	Maureen Lee and Mark Busto

WE ARE GRATEFUL FOR THE MAJOR SUPPORT PROVIDED BY:

Lannan

OFFICE OF ARTS & CULTURE

SEATTLE

Brice Marden

Ellie Mathews and Carl Youngmann
as The North Press

H. Stewart Parker

Penny and Jerry Peabody

John Phillips and Anne O'Donnell

Joseph C. Roberts

Cynthia Lovelace Sears and
Frank Buxton

The Seattle Foundation

Kim and Jeff Seely

David and Catherine Eaton Skinner

Dan Waggoner

C.D. Wright and Forrest Gander

Charles and Barbara Wright

The dedicated interns and faithful
volunteers of Copper Canyon Press

TO LEARN MORE ABOUT UNDERWRITING COPPER CANYON PRESS TITLES,
PLEASE CALL 360-385-4925 EXT. 103

The Chinese character for poetry is made up of two parts:
"word" and "temple." It also serves as pressmark for
Copper Canyon Press.

The poems are set in Adobe Garamond.
Printed on archival-quality paper.
Book design and composition by Phil Kovacevich.